PET GUIDE

Care for Your Kitten

Contents

HarperCollins*Publishers*
1 London Bridge Street
London SE1 9GF

www.harpercollins.co.uk

10 9 8 7 6 5 4 3 2 1

First published 1985 as *Care for your Kitten* by William Collins Sons & Co Ltd

This new edition published 2015

Front cover image: RSPCA
Photographs: RSPCA except for Africa Studio/Shutterstock.com p19; Alena Ozerova/Shutterstock.com p34; Anastasija Popova/Shutterstock.com p31 (bottom); Andrew Forsyth/RSPCA; p4, 27, 40 (right), 45; Becky Murray/RSPCA p5, 9 (right), 17 (top and bottom), 21, 23, 28 (top), 33, 35, 43 (top), 44 (top); Cherry Merry/Shutterstock.com p41; Digitalienspb/Shutterstock.com p8 (far right); Digitalienspb/Shutterstock.com p 9 (left); Dja65/Shutterstock.com p43 (below); Dmitrij Skorobogatov/Shutterstock.com p44 (below); Gurinaleksandr/Shutterstock.com p36; Jagodka/Shutterstock.com (centre) p9; Jagodka/Shutterstock.com p8 (left); Joe Murphy/RSPCA p6, 7, 8 (far left), 10 (top and bottom right), 39, 40 (left); Kalmatsuy/Shutterstock.com p8 (right); Karramba Production/Shutterstock.com p42 (right); Konrad Mostert/Shutterstock.com p30; Lars Kastilan/Shutterstock.com p24; Lili Chin/doggiedrawings.net p36, 37; Maximult/Shutterstock.com p25; Philip Toscano/RSPCA p10 (bottom left and top left); Rissy Story/Shutterstock.com p15; Tony Campbell/Shutterstock.com p16
Additional illustrations: Lili Chin @ www.doggiedrawings.net

This book has been compiled on the basis of expert advice and scientific research. To the best of our knowledge it is correct at the time of going to press. The information contained in this book is intended only as a guide. If you are unsure, or you have any concerns about your pet(s), you must speak to a vet, who will be able to give you advice that is appropriate for your individual animal(s).

The Animal Welfare Act 2006 applies to England and Wales. Similar separate legislation covers Scotland and Northern Ireland, so owners must fulfil the same legal duties of care.

PB ISBN 978-0-00-811829-7

Colour reproduction by Born

Printed and bound by South China Printing Company Ltd

MIX
Paper from
responsible sources
FSC™ C007454

FSC™ is a non-profit international organisation established to promote the responsible management of the world's forests. Products carrying the FSC label are independently certified to assure consumers that they come from forests that are managed to meet the social, economic and ecological needs of present and future generations, and other controlled sources.

Find out more about HarperCollins and the environment at
www.harpercollins.co.uk/green

Foreword

Owning a kitten can be incredibly rewarding and a great source of companionship. Pets can provide opportunities for social interactions, helping people feel less lonely and isolated. Growing up with pets also offers health benefits, and caring for an animal can help improve a child's social skills, encouraging the development of compassion, understanding and a respect for living things. Having a kitten is, however, a huge responsibility and requires long-term commitment in terms of care and finances.

Before getting a kitten, it is important that time is taken to discuss the commitment and care required with all family members, and that everyone agrees to having and looking after a kitten in the home. Bear in mind that once you have your kitten there is a legal requirement under the Animal Welfare Act 2006 to care for them properly, so you must be sure that you will be able to do this throughout your kitten's life. This means providing somewhere suitable for them to live, a healthy diet, opportunities to behave normally, the provision of appropriate company, and ensuring that they are well.

If you are able to care for a kitten properly and make the decision to go ahead, then please consider giving a home to one of the many kittens currently in the RSPCA's animal centres throughout England and Wales.

This book is based on up-to-date knowledge of cat behaviour and welfare approved by the RSPCA. It has been written to provide you with all the care information you need to keep your kitten happy and healthy throughout your lives together. We hope you enjoy it.

Samantha Gaines BSc (Hons) MSc PhD
Alice Potter BSc (Hons) MSc
Lisa Richards BSc (Hons)
Jane Tyson BSc (Hons) MSc PhD
Animal behaviour and welfare experts, Companion Animals
Department, RSPCA

Introduction

Owning and caring for a cat can be great fun and very rewarding. But it is also a big responsibility and a long-term commitment in terms of care and cost. Typically cats live for around 14 years, but some may live much longer, so before you get a kitten here are some of the things you need to consider:

Keeping a cat is costly

There is the initial expense of buying the kitten and everything they need, such as toys, bedding and litter. There are also long-term costs you should budget for, including food, insurance, veterinary care, neutering, vaccinations and the cost of catteries or pet sitters when you go on holiday.

Cats need space

Cats need space to exercise, climb, explore and rest undisturbed. Ideally most cats should have access to a garden or outdoor area where they can move around safely. They also need to be able to get back into the house at all times, day or night. One way that cats exercise is by scratching – you will need to provide scratching posts and should be aware that your kitten may damage carpets and furnishings.

Cats need company

Cats enjoy and benefit from human company. Can you be around so your kitten is not left alone for long periods, and can you allow enough time each day for feeding, playing and grooming?

The right type of cat for your family

Take time to find out which type of cat will fit best into your family's lifestyle. While you may have a preference about the breed or sex, remember that every cat is unique. How a kitten behaves and fits into your family will depend on how they are treated and trained, as well as their individual character and temperament.

The Animal Welfare Act

Under the Animal Welfare Act 2006 it is a legal obligation to care for animals properly by meeting five welfare needs. These are: a suitable place to live, a healthy diet including clean, fresh water, the ability to behave normally, appropriate company and protection from pain, suffering, injury and illness. This care guide contains lots of information and tips to help you make sure these needs are met.

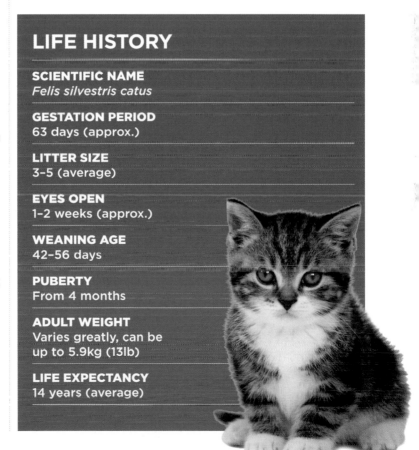

LIFE HISTORY

SCIENTIFIC NAME
Felis silvestris catus

GESTATION PERIOD
63 days (approx.)

LITTER SIZE
3–5 (average)

EYES OPEN
1–2 weeks (approx.)

WEANING AGE
42–56 days

PUBERTY
From 4 months

ADULT WEIGHT
Varies greatly, can be up to 5.9kg (13lb)

LIFE EXPECTANCY
14 years (average)

Choosing the right type of cat for you

If you are certain that you will be able to care for a kitten, the next stage is to do plenty of research to decide which type of cat is right for you.

Sex

All cats are individuals, and there are no significant differences between male and female kittens, so both can make excellent pets. What sex you choose is a personal decision.

Whether you choose a male or a female, it is best to have your cat neutered. You may hear this referred to as being 'fixed', 'done' or 'spayed' for a female cat, or 'snipped' for a male cat. Cats can reach sexual maturity at 4 months old, at which time female cats can get pregnant and will start to attract a lot of unwanted attention from nearby male cats. It is important to have her spayed before this time to protect her from getting pregnant while she is still a kitten herself. You may have heard that it is good for cats to have a litter of kittens before they are spayed, but this isn't true. Once she has been spayed, your female kitten will be able to do all the things cats enjoy doing, like going outdoors, climbing trees and playing.

Your boy cat will need to have a simple operation called the snip. This can stop him from spraying in your house to mark his territory, which can be very smelly, and getting nasty injuries from fights. He will also be less likely to wander off and get run over, as cats that are snipped tend to stay closer to home.

Purebred or crossbreed

Once you've decided on the sex of your cat, your next decision should be whether you want a purebred (the cat's parents are both the same single breed) or a crossbreed (a mix of two or more breeds). There are advantages to both purebreds and crossbreeds, and your decision may depend upon your personal preference, situation and the circumstances of the kittens you are considering. When purchasing kittens

that the breeders have registered as pedigrees, you will have a better idea of their parentage and what to expect in terms of their adult appearance. Genetic testing may also have been carried out to ensure that the kittens are not predisposed to particular conditions. On the other hand, crossbreeds are less likely to show the exaggerated physical features and inherited diseases that are present in particular breeds, although they can still inherit disorders from their parents' breeds. They also generally cost less to buy and are cheaper to insure. Most cats in the United Kingdom are crossbreeds, so they are much more widely available.

Whatever type of cat you're thinking of getting, it is important to find out what health and physical issues the breed may be vulnerable to developing. As well as causing pain and suffering to your kitten, such propensities to specific problems may also lead to expensive bills for veterinary treatment throughout their lives. Knowing which types of cat tend to have fewer problems will give you the best chance of getting a happy, healthy kitten.

TOP LEFT: Both male and female kittens make excellent pets. LEFT: Most cats in the UK are crossbreeds.

Types of cat

There is a variety of different types of cat; below are some examples.

Crossbreed

A crossbred cat is often called a 'moggy'. Moggies are not one particular breed but can be made up of a mixture of two or more breeds. This means they come in a variety of different shapes, sizes, colours and markings. Although you will not be as sure of how a moggy kitten will look when they grow up, you can be sure that, like all cats, they will bring love and enjoyment into your life.

Shorthair

There are many breeds of cat classed as 'Shorthairs'. British Shorthairs have short, dense fur; other Shorthair varieties include the Selkirk Rex, which has a somewhat woolly coat; the tailless Manx cat, which originated in the Isle of Man; and the Scottish Fold, which is a similar size to the British Shorthair but has forward-folded ears.

Foreign Shorthair

These cats come from all over the world. Each type tends to be fairly slender, having longer faces than British Shorthairs, large ears and long, slim tails. Abyssinian cats are thought to resemble the cats of ancient Egypt, the Russian Blue has a short, dense, slate-grey coat, while the Korat cat is named after a province in Thailand.

There are two varieties of Rex cats, the Cornish Rex and the Devon Rex, both of which have curly coats. They are named after the English counties where they were first discovered.

Other Foreign Shorthair varieties include the Australian Mist, Bengal, Egyptian Mau, Singapura, Snowshoe, Havana Brown and Tonkinese. The Sphynx appears to have no fur at all, though they actually have a fine layer of downy hair.

LEFT TO RIGHT:
Crossbreed,
Shorthair, Foreign
Shorthair, Semi-
longhair, Burmese,
Siamese, Persian.

Semi-longhair

Some cat breeds are classed as 'Semi-longhairs'. These include the Birman, which has white paws and white lower legs, the Ragdoll and the Balinese. Maine Coon cats are the largest of all cat breeds and come from the United States. Other Semi-longhair varieties include the Norwegian Forest cat, the Siberian, the Somali – a longer-haired version of the well-known Abyssinian cat – and the Ragamuffin.

Burmese

This is a medium-sized breed with a short coat, sturdy body and, typically, yellow eyes. They are believed to have originated in Myanmar (formerly Burma). There are many variations in the colours of their coats. Another variety, the Bombay, is bred from Burmese and black Shorthair cats.

Siamese and Oriental

The coat colour of Siamese cats is defined by the 'points' – the face (or mask), the ears, the legs and paws and the tail. All Siamese cats tend to have short coats and blue eyes. Orientals are cats derived from Siamese cats and are similar in appearance, except they generally have green eyes.

Persian or Longhair

The Persian, known for its long coat, is thought to be one of the oldest breeds of cat. Long-haired cats, which are believed to have first been seen in Europe in the 16th century, are thought to have originated in Turkey and were originally called Angora cats – after the city of Ankara. Later, other long-haired cats were brought from Persia and the name Persian stuck.

Getting a kitten

Where to buy

Although you may have decided which size, sex and type of cat is most suitable for your family, you should take your time in selecting the right individual kitten.

The RSPCA encourages anyone looking for a pet to consider taking on one of the thousands of animals it rescues each year. Rehoming charities have kittens of all different types and colours looking

for a good home.

If you are planning to buy your kitten directly from the person who bred them, do some research first to make sure you choose a responsible breeder. Breeders should be happy to discuss with you subjects such as how the kittens have been kept, and should invite you to visit their home. This is important because, wherever possible, you should try to see the kittens with their mothers, as this will give you a good picture of how well they have been cared for, and seeing the parent will give you a fair indication of the kitten's eventual size and sociability.

Avoid advertisements that invite you to meet the breeder at a location other than the place where the kittens were born. You will not be able to check the kitten's origins, nor will you be able to see the kitten with its littermates and parents to see how they behave and if they are all healthy.

Meeting a kitten

When you are choosing a kitten, look for signs that the cats seem healthy and well cared for. If the kittens seem nervous or timid, they may not have had enough chances to socialize, which could mean that they will be scared or anxious as they grow older. If you have any doubts about a litter, it is best not to choose one of them as your pet. Never pick a timid kitten because you feel sorry for them. Wherever you get your kitten, you should collect them when they have been be weaned and are old enough to be separated from their mother (generally this is at least 8 weeks old).

Finding a healthy kitten

It is important to make sure your kitten is healthy before you take them home. Here are some things that may signal health problems:

- Visible ribs or a bloated tummy
- Runny eyes
- Coughing
- A sore bottom, wet tail or yellow stains on the fur (signs of diarrhoea)
- A dull, scruffy coat
- Signs of parasites such as fleas or ear mites. Look for scratching, areas of hair loss, or dark grey or brown deposits in the ears
- Weakness, wobbliness or difficulty standing up
- Becoming tired very quickly on interaction or play
- Noisy or laboured breathing
- Limping, difficulty walking or lifting legs
- A prolonged hunched or crouched body posture
- Straining when passing urine or faeces

These are just a few examples. If you notice anything at all that doesn't look quite right with the kitten you have seen, you may want to consider getting your pet from somewhere else. If you have concerns about any of the animals you have seen, call the RSPCA (details can be found at www.rspca.org.uk).

CLOCKWISE FROM TOP LEFT: Consider visiting a rescue organization such as the RSPCA. Check the kitten is healthy. Make sure you see a kitten with its littermates and parents. Rescue organizations have many cats and kittens waiting to be rehomed.

Biology

Movement
A kitten's skeleton is extraordinarily flexible, which is what makes cats such agile animals. Their tail helps them with movement, acting as a balancing mechanism when the kitten is climbing or jumping; it also provides warmth during sleep and acts as a signalling device. A kitten will often greet familiar people with their tail held high and the tip pointing forwards.

Claws
A kitten's claws are crucial for defence, scratching and as an aid to climbing. Claws are made of keratin, the same substance that forms skin, so they are counted as part of the cat's skin rather than their skeleton. Kittens should not need to have their claws trimmed – normal use will keep them at their proper length.

Ears
Cats have super-sensitive hearing. Most of a cat's ear is hidden within the skull; the ear flap, or 'pinna', funnels sound waves down into the ear drum and from there into the inner ear. The ears can also be used as a means of expression – they change position according to how the cat is feeling.

Eyes
Kittens are born with their eyes closed; they begin to open when the kitten is between one and two weeks old. Kittens are typically born with blue eyes, but at around 12 weeks the adult colour begins to emerge. Cats have a wide variety of eye colours, ranging through orange, copper, yellow, hazel, green and blue. Kittens do not see as well as adult cats until they are about 3 months old.

Whiskers
Most kittens are born with a full set of whiskers – these are found on the sides of the nose, cheeks and above the eyes. Whiskers are well supplied with nerve endings and so are very sensitive to touch. A cat's whiskers are very important – they help them to sense where obstacles are in the dark and to gauge distances between objects.

Teeth
Kittens are born with 'baby' teeth, which start to be shed at around 12 weeks. The full set of 30 teeth has generally grown in by about 7 months. It consists of 12 incisors, 4 canines, 10 premolars and 4 molars. A cat's teeth should be checked regularly for problems or signs of infection – your vet can show you how to do this.

Tongue

A cat's long, muscular, agile tongue is an essential grooming aid. The middle of the tongue is covered with small projections, called 'papillae', that give it its characteristic sandpapery feel. The tongue is also vital for lapping water.

Exaggerated features

Many breeds have been bred to emphasize certain physical features, which over time have become more exaggerated. Although these may be 'normal' for a specific breed, flat faces, short legs and exaggerated eye shapes are just a few examples of features that may cause problems to the animal's health. For example, cats with short, flat faces can suffer severe breathing difficulties. Cats with exaggerated eye shapes can be prone to glaucoma, which is painful and leads to a progressive loss of vision. Some of these problems will require lifelong medication or sometimes surgery. Try to ensure that any kitten you choose is free from exaggerated features.

Environment

1

Your kitten needs safe, suitable places to hide and relax.

A suitable place to live

Before you bring your kitten home, make sure you have prepared a suitable, safe place for them to live in and that you have everything they will need to be happy and well looked after. Here are some things to consider:

A secure, comfortable space

For the first few days, it is best to confine your kitten to just one room, where they can feel secure while getting used to the new surroundings. The room should be free of hazards like trailing electrical wires and open windows.

A suitable bed

Your kitten will need a comfortable place to rest and relax. Always look for a bed that is big enough to allow them to lie comfortably in natural positions, such as with their legs extended, or curled up. As well as being soft and padded, the bed should also be durable, washable and easy to dry so you can keep it clean. Make sure it is made of material that is safe for your cat.

No matter how carefully you choose a bed, you may find that your kitten prefers a different place to sleep – very ▶

◀ possibly your bed! If you don't want your cat sleeping there, you can prevent this simply by keeping your door closed.

Somewhere to feel safe

Even after they are ready to explore the rest of the house, your kitten will need places to hide from time to time. Cats hide when they feel frightened or insecure, so providing cats and kittens with safe places to retreat helps them cope with fear or anxiety and gives them somewhere to relax. You can make a great hiding place by filling a box with soft bedding and cutting an entrance and exit hole that is big enough for your cat. You can also purchase igloo-type cat beds. Make sure you position the hiding place in a quiet part of your house so that your cat is never disturbed whilst in there.

Playtime

Make sure your kitten has enough space to exercise, climb and play indoors. Kittens are born with a hunting instinct and will enjoy playing with objects they can 'attack', like balls and toy mice. Avoid letting your kitten 'attack' your hands or any part of your body when they are playing – if a kitten learns this is OK they may do the same as an adult, which can be very painful.

Play will help keep your kitten mentally alert and physically fit, and will prevent them getting bored. Most cats enjoy chasing, so try throwing a small, soft object across the floor. Use simple string-and-stick toys with something mouse-like at the end, and encourage your cat to stalk, chase and grab the toy. Be sure to let them actually grab it at some point, or they may get frustrated.

RIGHT: Toys can help your kitten to stay mentally alert and physically fit. ABOVE RIGHT: Choose a soft, padded bed for your kitten. BOTTOM RIGHT: Choose a quiet spot for your kitten's litter tray.

Choose toys for your kitten with care. Make sure they are suitably sized, to minimize the risk of swallowing or choking, avoid any with sharp edges and always remove and replace them when they are damaged.

Litter tray

Cats need to go to the toilet regularly, either outdoors or in a litter tray placed well away from where they eat and sleep. They also like some privacy, so position a tray away from any noisy parts of the house. If you have more than one cat, they should each have their own litter tray.

The litter tray should be sturdy and leak-proof. Bigger is always better – it should be big enough for the cat to turn around in comfortably, and the litter should be deep enough for the cat to be able to dig and cover up their faeces. Any mess should be scooped out as often as possible, and the entire litter tray should be emptied and cleaned regularly. Cats do not like using a dirty litter tray.

When choosing cleaning products for your cat's litter tray, try to avoid anything heavily scented, such as fragranced litter or very strong-smelling cleaner. Cats can be very sensitive to strong smells and it may put them off using their litter tray. Make sure all cleaning products are safe for your cat – avoid bleach or household cleaning solutions; they may contain coal tar and carbolic derivatives, which are poisonous to cats.

If you have a garden, you may find that after a time your kitten prefers going outside to using the litter tray. However, it may still be a good idea to keep the litter tray available in case of bad weather.

If your cat ever urinates or defecates outside the litter tray (or in the house, if they are used to going outside), this may be a sign of illness or stress. Never punish your cat for this behaviour, and always consult your vet to rule out health problems.

Inside and out

Until your kitten is confident and secure in their surroundings, it is best not to let them out without supervision. When your kitten has settled in and is fully vaccinated, they will be ready to go out and explore the garden and the wider world. Make sure your garden is escape-proof and free of hazards before you let them out, and keep a close watch. They should have access to the house at all times of the day and night, so a cat flap fitted to a convenient external door will be useful. Sometimes the outside world can seem a bit threatening to a ▶

Once your kitten is settled and fully vaccinated they can explore outside.

cat – sudden bad weather, the presence of other cats and loud noises can frighten or upset them – so make sure they can easily beat a safe retreat back to the security of home and can get into the house at any time.

It is not recommended that you keep a cat permanently indoors if they have been used to going outside, unless your vet has advised otherwise. But if cats are kept in from an early age, some can adapt to an indoor life.

If your cat doesn't have the freedom to go outside, you still need to provide everything they need to stay healthy and happy. Make sure they have enough space to exercise, climb and play indoors, and include a variety of resting places for them to use. Remember, cats are intelligent so they can get bored if they don't have enough to do! Indoor cats need the same physical and mental stimulation as outdoor cats, so give your cat lots of care and attention every day.

Holiday time

Cats become very attached to familiar places, so if you are going away, asking a familiar friend or family member to look after your cat at home can be the least stressful option for your pet. If no one is available, you can arrange for a pet sitter to come into your home. Anyone who looks after your cat while you are away should have clear instructions on your cat's dietary needs, any medication they should have, a contact number for you, and your vet's phone number in case of an emergency.

If you are planning to board your pet, make sure the cattery is licensed by the local council. You should always visit the cattery ahead of time to make sure that your cat will be in secure, clean, dry and draught-free surroundings that are attended at all times. Do the other animals boarding there look clean, happy and healthy? Good catteries will insist that all cats are fully vaccinated and will ask to see certificates. Boarding can be stressful for cats, so to help your cat feel more at home, bring along their bed and some favourite toys.

On the move

For trips to the cattery or to the vet you will need a suitable carrier for your cat. It should be large enough for your cat to sit, lie and turn around in comfortably. You may find it helpful to choose a carrier with a side and top opening, as this can make access easier. Your cat should be able to see out, and there must be adequate ventilation so that they can breathe. For safety, the carrier should be robust, durable and made from materials that are safe for cats. Whichever one you choose, make sure it will hold your kitten securely in your vehicle. You may need to replace the carrier as your cat grows.

It can get unbearably hot in a car on a sunny day, even when it is not that warm outside, so be aware of this when you are transporting your kitten. Do not leave them alone in a vehicle, as the temperature can quickly soar to unbearable levels, which can be fatal.

Moving house

If you move house, try to keep your cat away from the commotion of packing, unpacking, moving and cleaning.

Designate one room in your house for your cat and put everything they will need in there, including food, water, litter tray and bed. The evening before moving day, feed your cat in the room, then shut the door to stop them disappearing. On the day of the move, leave your cat in the room until the rest of the house has been packed up, then put them into a carrier for the journey to your new home.

Once you have moved, your cat may try to go back to your previous home, so it is best to keep them indoors for at least two weeks. Make sure your cat is microchipped and that the stored information is updated with your new address. Supervising your cat the first few times they venture out will be reassuring for you both.

Choose a carrier with a side and top opening for easy access.

Diet

2

Place your kitten's food and water bowls in separate areas.

What to feed your kitten

A healthy diet

In order to stay fit and healthy, your kitten needs a well-balanced diet and access to clean, fresh drinking water at all times. The amount you feed your cat will depend on their age, level of activity and general health. If cats eat too much or too little, their health will suffer. Your vet is the best person to advise you on how much and what kind of food is best for your kitten.

Bowls

Before bringing your kitten home, you will need to buy bowls for food and water. These should be made of a hard, durable material like metal or ceramic and must be replaced if they become damaged.

The bowls should be easy to clean and large and shallow enough to allow your cat to eat and drink without their whiskers touching the sides of the bowl. You should have separate bowls for food and water, not one divided bowl. It is important to place your cat's food and water bowls in separate areas, as cats do not like to drink near where they eat. If you have more than one cat, make sure each cat has their own bowl. These should be placed in different areas for each cat.

Place your cat's bowls away from the litter tray, and make sure the food bowl is clean and dry before your cat is fed.

Types of food

Kittens should be fed a weighed or measured amount of food at regular times. Cat food can be wet or dry, and what is suitable will depend on your individual kitten's needs. Mealtimes should always be supervised. Whatever prepared food you choose, always read the manufacturer's instructions. Cats are naturally meat-eaters and are not suited to a vegetarian diet, so they need a meat-based diet in order to stay fit and healthy.

Do not feed your cat dog food; it does not have all the ingredients your cat or kitten needs. You should also avoid giving your cat table scraps, as many 'human' foods can be poisonous to cats. Foods that can cause illness or even death in cats include dairy products, chocolate, caffeine, grapes, raisins, onions and garlic. Also avoid giving your cat bones, as these can be a choking hazard and can damage the intestines if swallowed.

How much and how often?

Kittens have small stomachs so they need to be fed little and often. Feed your kitten every day, splitting the daily ration into several small meals throughout the day. The number of meals they have will depend on your kitten's age – speak to your vet about what is right for your cat. If your cat's eating and drinking habits change, talk to your vet, as your pet could be ill.

Even when your kitten becomes an adult cat it can still be best to feed them several small meals. Giving your cat one large bowl of food a day that is always available can lead to boredom and lack of activity, which can in turn make your cat overweight. Cats' needs can vary, so ask your vet for advice on how often and how much to feed.

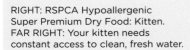

RIGHT: RSPCA Hypoallergenic Super Premium Dry Food: Kitten.
FAR RIGHT: Your kitten needs constant access to clean, fresh water.

ABOVE: Treats can be used to reward your cat during training.
TOP RIGHT: Your vet can show you how to perform weight checks.

Drink up!

Your kitten will need constant access to fresh, clean water, so you will need to keep a close eye on their water bowl to ensure that it is kept topped up.

Many cats like to drink from a running water source – some will drink straight from the tap if they have the chance. In the wild, cats prefer a running stream over a stagnant pool because the water is fresher. If you want to give your cat running water, you may be able to find a cat water fountain in your local pet shop.

Cats should not drink cow's milk. Cats

are lactose intolerant, which means they lack the enzyme needed to digest milk properly. Milk can therefore give cats diarrhoea and cause digestive problems in adulthood. It is much safer and healthier to give your cat water only.

The first few days

Usually, a breeder or rescue centre will provide information about a kitten's diet, telling you what type of food they have been eating so far and how often. Whenever possible, keep your kitten's food and feeding routine the same while they are settling in. Any changes in a kitten's diet should only be made gradually, as a sudden swap in brand or type of food can lead to an upset stomach. When changing a kitten's diet, do it over several days; gradually replace the food they are used to with increasing amounts of the new food each day.

Treats

Many owners enjoy giving their cats treats from time to time – feeding your cat a tasty tidbit by hand is one way to show affection and can help strengthen your bond. Treats can also be used to reward your cat during training.

There are many commercially available cat treats. Consider carefully how many treats you are giving your cat, as they add extra calories that can lead to weight problems. If you give your cat a treat, reduce their main meal slightly to avoid overfeeding.

WEIGHT WATCHING

Ensuring your cat doesn't become overweight is essential for their health and requires a combination of a healthy diet and regular exercise. A cat that is a healthy weight is likely to live longer, have more energy and be more resistant to disease than one that is allowed to become overweight.

Cats come in many shapes and sizes, and some are naturally bigger or smaller than average. Sometimes it is tricky to see a cat's true body shape as it may be disguised by their coat, but there are a number of more visible signs that will indicate if your cat is at their ideal weight.

- You should be able to feel your cat's ribs without excess fat covering.
- When you look at your cat from above, you should see a clear waistline.
- When you look at your cat from the side, you should see only a slight belly.

If your cat does not pass all three checks, or if you are in any doubt about their weight, talk to your vet. For further information about pet obesity visit the RSPCA website at www.rspca.org.uk/pets.

Behaviour

3

A kitten exploring an RSPCA rehoming pod.

Kitten behaviour

Kittens are active, energetic and playful, and should be given the freedom to behave normally by jumping, climbing and exploring their home territory. They often enjoy having fun with toys and people. Kittens use lots of energy throughout the day, so they also need plenty of sleep in a safe, quiet place where they will not be disturbed by children or the household routine.

Socialization and habituation

The first 8 weeks of a kitten's life are a critical time; this is when they learn how to interact with their environment, people and other animals. Kittens who are well socialized during the first few weeks of their life, by being handled gently and exposed gradually to contact with humans and other animals, are more likely to be well-adjusted, happy and healthy cats. ▶

◀ Kittens also need to be gradually introduced to a full range of normal household sounds and objects that they will encounter in their new homes, such as vacuum cleaners, so that they learn not to be afraid of them.

Exercise

All cats need to be able to exercise regularly and have plenty of opportunities to run, play, jump, climb and scratch. Cats are natural climbers, so make sure they have elevated spaces they can reach safely – these are also valuable safe resting places that your cats can go to if they are frightened or uncomfortable, or just want to view their surroundings from up high.

Cats that have outdoor access generally have more space to move around than those that live indoors only. If your cat lives indoors it is important that they have access to several rooms, if not the entire house. Cats that live indoors may also need extra encouragement to exercise. Find out what toys your cat likes and spend plenty of time every day playing games that encourage them to be active.

TOP: An older kitten who has been well socialized from an early age. ABOVE: Any opportunity for outdoor exercise is very important for kittens. Try to make time to play with your kitten in the garden. FAR RIGHT: Scratching strengthens your kitten's muscles and is good for the claws, too.

Playing with food!

Food toys encourage physical activity in indoor cats and help prevent boredom. A treat ball filled with dry food will encourage your cat to roll and chase it until the food falls out. A Kitty Kong toy is best for this game if you feed your cat wet food. You can make cat-food toys out of stacked kitchen roll tubes with bits of food inside each one, or an empty biscuit tray with food sprinkled in some of the sections. Your cat will need to use their paws to get the food out.

Of course, if you use food toys, be sure you take into account the extra calories you are giving them and adjust your cat's daily food intake accordingly.

Training your cat

Contrary to popular belief, kittens and cats can be trained to follow commands such as 'sit', to come when called and even to high-five! Cats should always be trained using positive rewards.

One of the most important things you can train a kitten to do is feel relaxed and comfortable in their carrier. Many adult cats experience a great deal of stress when they are put into a carrier; many have to be forced inside because they are too fearful to enter willingly. This can be a stressful experience for you as a cat owner, too. However, there are ways to help make cats feel more comfortable, and if you take these steps while your cat is still a kitten, they will learn early on that carriers are safe places. ▶

WHY DO CATS SCRATCH?

Scratching is a natural behaviour for cats. It keeps their claws in good condition and strengthens their muscles, as well as allowing them to scent mark using the glands between their toe-pads.

Scratching posts can be covered in various materials; most commonly they are clad in sisal, carpet or corrugated cardboard. Many cats seem to prefer something with a vertical thread, which helps them get a good grip and 'pull'. Make sure your kitten's scratching posts are solid and heavy enough so that they don't topple over, and tall enough so that your kitten can stretch up fully. If your kitten does start scratching furniture, try placing a scratching post in front of the place they scratch, such as the corner of a sofa, for example. Cats like to scratch and stretch after they have been sleeping, so placing the post next to their favourite sleeping spot can encourage them to use it. Indoor cats often have fewer suitable scratching places than outdoor cats and may start scratching furniture, wallpaper or carpets, so it is vital to provide at least one suitable scratching post.

Soft bedding and treats can encourage your kitten to get used to a carrier.

◀ Leave the cat carrier out at all times so that your cat becomes familiar with it. Make it cosy by placing some soft bedding inside, and leave it open in a quiet part of the house so that your cat can investigate and go inside – they may even choose to have a little snooze in there. After a while the carrier should start to smell familiar and feel more comfortable to your cat.

You can also use food to make the carrier friendlier. Regularly place small tasty treats inside to encourage your kitten to go in there willingly and in their own time.

Playing games around the carrier can also help kittens to become more comfortable with it. Using a rod and string toy, slowly lure your kitten towards the carrier, then move the toy to encourage your kitten to run around it, jump on top of it and hide behind it. Your kitten should begin to associate the carrier with fun and games.

The pros and cons of collars

Cats are not legally required to wear collars. However, owners have various reasons for wanting their cats to wear them. Some owners attach an identity tag, in case their cat gets lost. Cats who are out at night, especially those with dark fur, will be more visible in car headlights if they are wearing a reflective collar. Some cat flaps work by means of a magnetic device attached to a collar.

If your cat is a keen hunter, a collar with a bell attached can warn prey of their approach and may help to protect the wildlife in your area.

Badly designed or ill-fitting collars can be dangerous, so if you choose to have your cat wear a collar, make sure it is fitted with a quick-release safety buckle that snaps open when pressure is applied, so that the collar will just fall off. Elasticated collars are not suitable, as it is too easy for the cat to get their front leg caught and trapped in the collar, or for the collar to snag on something and leave your cat unable to escape. When you fit a collar on your cat, make sure it is not too tight – you should be able to get one or two fingers under it. Check it regularly and replace the collar as soon as it starts to fray or wear out.

If you are concerned about your cat getting lost, make sure they are microchipped so that you don't need to rely on a collar for identification.

When there are problems

The way a cat behaves depends on their age, type, personality and past experiences – frightening experiences and punishment can lead to behaviour problems and suffering. Never shout at or punish your cat, as they are very unlikely to understand and can become more nervous or scared. Signs that a cat may be suffering from stress or fear can include high levels of grooming, hiding, sleeping in a hunched posture and altered feeding or toileting habits. Cats that are frightened or in pain may change their behaviour or develop unwanted behaviours such as aggression, spraying indoors, over-grooming or avoiding people. You should make sure your kitten has constant access to a safe hiding place to escape to if they feel afraid.

If your kitten's behaviour changes, it could mean they are distressed, bored, ill or injured, so always talk to your vet if you are concerned. If necessary, your vet can refer you to a clinical animal behaviourist. For further information on clinical animal behaviourists, see page 47.

TOP: Cats need plenty of opportunities to run, jump, play and scratch. ABOVE: Excessive grooming can be a sign of stress or fear.

Company

4

Most cats prefer their head and neck to be stroked.

Being with others

If cats are treated well when they are kittens, they can learn to see people as companions.

Cats are often viewed as solitary animals, but many enjoy and benefit from company, including that of humans. Though they are happy to spend some time on their own, being left alone all day can be stressful for them so make sure you spend some time with your cat each day. Playing with your kitten can help strengthen your bond, and your kitten's best playtime toy is you! Even if you are not playing together, sitting nearby and reading while they snooze in a chair or in their bed is a way of offering companionship.

When you are away

Cats are generally independent, but they should never be left alone to look after themselves while you are away for any length of time. If you have to be away overnight or longer and want to leave your cat at home rather than in a cattery, always ask a responsible adult to come in to feed them and check that they are well. The carer should also spend a little time playing or interacting with your cat if possible.

KITTENS AND CHILDREN

Having a pet can improve a child's social skills, and caring for an animal can encourage kindness, understanding and responsibility. While children will quickly learn to treat a new kitten as part of the family, it is important to teach them to stay safe around cats, and to make sure the kitten stays safe as well.

If your children are very young, it is best not to leave them alone with your new kitten right away. Kittens can be rough when they play – scratching and biting is how they interact with their siblings.

Children also need to be shown how to be gentle with kittens. Teach them the right way to handle your pet and the importance of not holding the kitten too tightly or pulling their tail, whiskers or any other body part. Kittens and cats should never be dressed up, as this can be stressful for them.

Cats need lots of rest, so children – and adults – should never force a cat to play, or disturb a cat that is sleeping or eating. If a cat moves away from you or hides, they may be stressed and should be left alone; if the cat is forced to interact, they may become aggressive.

Showing affection

It is natural to want to show your cat affection by cuddling them. Though you might enjoy giving your kitten big hugs or belly rubs, your kitten may not appreciate them. When cats groom each other, they focus on the head and neck, and prefer, when people stroke them, that they concentrate on these areas, too.

Cats groom one another as a sign of affection, so spending time grooming your cat is a way of offering companionship and strengthening your bond. See pages 41–2 for advice on how to groom your cat.

Typically, cats will let you know when they want your attention – they may miaow, rub against you, sit close to you or even climb into your lap. So take your cue from your kitten and let them approach you before treating them to a gentle chin, cheek and head rub.

Holding and handling

It is important for everyone in the family, especially children, to learn the right way to handle a kitten. Cats and kittens should never be forced to interact with people if they don't want to – if they show signs of being worried or unhappy (see page 31) any handling should stop. Cats and kittens should never be picked up by the scruff of the neck. Many cats don't enjoy being picked up at all and feel more secure when they have four feet on the ground – a head stroke or chin rub is often a better way to show your affection. If you do lift your pet, be

sure to support their weight and hold them safely using both hands. A kitten that is held properly and gently from an early age is more likely to be happy to be picked up when they are older. It may help your kitten to enjoy being held if you give them a gentle stroke on the top of their head.

More than one cat?

Many cats are happier living without other cats. They can be social, but they prefer to choose their own companions. However, if cats are introduced appropriately and there is no competition for food or safe sleeping places, they can accept each other. If you want more than one cat, it is best to introduce them when they are both young or to adopt a sibling pair. If they are brought together as adults, they may be aggressive towards one another, which will be stressful for both cats.

Introducing a new kitten into a household that already has a cat should be done slowly and carefully. Each cat should have their own safe sleeping space, food and water bowls and litter tray. This will reduce competition and help them to live together more harmoniously.

TOP LEFT: Teach your children to be gentle with your kitten. TOP RIGHT: If cats are introduced appropriately they can learn to accept each other. RIGHT: Learn the right way to handle your kitten.

If possible, keep the cats in separate areas of the house for a few days at first, but allow each cat to investigate the other's room and bed without actually meeting. This will enable them to get accustomed to each other's scent.

When the cats do first meet, choose a room where they can escape behind furniture, jump up high, or hide if necessary. A qualified animal behaviourist (see page 47) can give you further advice on how to introduce a new cat into the household.

If, after a reasonable time, the cats still do not get along, make sure that they are both able to avoid each other at all times and that they can both access everything they need without having to interact. Cats should never be forced to socialize with other animals they dislike. For more information, go to www.rspca.org.uk/cats/company.

Cats and other pets

It is possible for cats to live with other pets, but certain factors should be taken into consideration, such as the temperaments and personalities of both animals. For example, a cat that has a nervous or timid personality may be less likely to cope with living with an energetic dog.

The way in which the pets are introduced is very important to how they will interact. Introducing the pets to each other slowly and gradually will make it more likely that they will live comfortably together. For further information about introducing cats to other pets, go to www.rspca.org.uk/cats/company.

Animals that are normally hunted and are prey to cats, such as birds, fish and small rodents, must be kept safely in secure enclosures that the cat cannot open, knock down or otherwise disturb.

Introduce your pets to each other slowly and gradually.

Body language

A happy cat

These cats are relaxed and happy.

1 Cat is standing up, relaxed body posture, ears in natural position, tail held upright with the tip of the tail curved, eyes normal shape, mouth closed.

2 Cat is lying down, belly exposed, body posture relaxed, body stretched out, ears in natural position, eyes may be partly closed, mouth closed.

3 Cat is sitting, body posture relaxed, tail held loosely from body, ears in natural position, eyes normal shape, mouth closed.

Your kitten's body language can help you to understand how they are feeling.

A worried cat
These cats are uncomfortable and don't want you near them.

1 Cat is in a crouched position, muscles tense, body held tightly, tail tucked tightly into body, ears slightly swivelled sideways, head slightly lowered and tucked into body, pupils dilated, mild tension shows in face.

2 Cats who are worried or anxious may hide.

An angry cat
These cats are not happy and want you to stay away or go away.

1 Cat is lying down, body flattened, ears flattened to head, pupils dilated, tail held tightly in, body tense, limbs held tight and close to body.

2 Cat is lying down, body flattened, ears flattened and drawn back, body slightly rolled over to one side, pupils dilated, mouth open and tense, teeth showing.

3 Cat is standing, back arched, body held sideways, hair raised, front paw slightly lifted, ears lowered and pointing sideways, teeth showing, tail tense.

Health
and welfare

5

Protecting your pet

Cats can suffer from a range of diseases and illnesses, and individual cats show pain and suffering in different ways. It may not be obvious that your kitten is suffering, because cats do not always show outward signs that they are ill or in pain. However, any change in the way your kitten behaves can indicate that they are unwell or in distress. Check your cat for signs of injury or illness every day, and make sure someone else does this if you are away.

Find a vet and arrange insurance

It is important that you register your new kitten with a vet as soon as possible and book them in for a check-up and vaccinations. You can read more about finding a vet and low-cost vet care at www.rspca.org.uk/whatwedo/vetcare.

Check the insurance situation, too. Some charities and breeders may provide a short period of insurance cover, which you can either take over and extend, or you may want to arrange an alternative policy. Where insurance is not provided, it is a good idea to arrange for a policy to start from the moment you bring home the kitten.

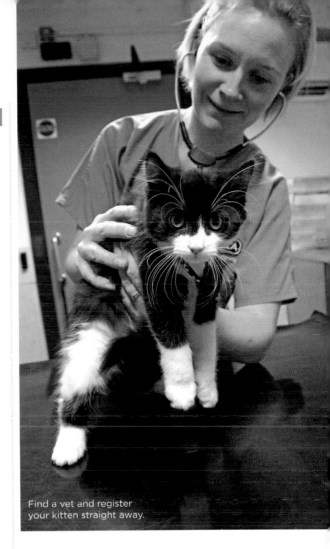
Find a vet and register your kitten straight away.

Health checks

Take your cat to the vet for a routine health check at least once a year. It is a good chance to ask for advice about what you can do to protect your cat's health, including essential vaccinations and treatments to control parasites (e.g. fleas and worms).

Microchipping

Microchipping your kitten gives them the best chance of being identified and returned to you if they are lost or stolen. ▶

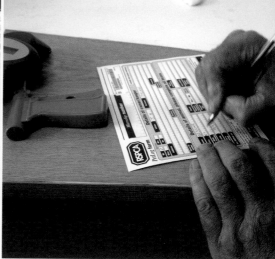

LEFT: Vaccinating your kitten gives protection against a number of diseases. ABOVE: Microchipping helps to ensure your kitten can be identified if they are lost or stolen.

◄ A tiny microchip containing a unique code is inserted under their skin; this can be scanned and matched to your contact details, which are held on a database, so make sure you keep your contact information up to date.

Vaccinations

Vaccinations are very important to prevent a number of deadly diseases. Kittens are usually vaccinated at around 8 or 9 weeks and again at 12 weeks, but you should speak to your vet for more information. When a kitten is vaccinated, the vet will provide a vaccination certificate that shows the date on which it was administered and the products used. For more information go to www.rspca.org.uk/pets.

Worming

Regular worming is important for all cats, as even healthy-looking animals can carry them. Ask your vet about the best treatment to use, and how often it should be given. Avoid buying your kitten from breeders who have not wormed their cats and kittens.

Fleas

If you notice your kitten scratching furiously, or if you have unexplained insect bites, your kitten may have fleas. Your vet will advise you of the most appropriate treatment for your cat's age and size. You must also wash bedding, vacuum furniture, floors and skirting boards and throw away the vacuum bag to get rid of any flea eggs. Flea problems must be tackled quickly, as they can infect your cats with the tapeworm parasite, as well as other diseases. Make sure your kitten is also wormed as part of the treatment.

Never use dog flea products on your kitten or cat, as it can be fatal. Dog flea products contain the insecticide permethrin, which is highly toxic to cats.

Always carefully check the packaging of any flea treatment you use. If any spot-on product containing permethrin is used on your cat, you must seek immediate treatment from a veterinary surgeon.

Grooming

Grooming should become part of your cat's regular routine. Grooming removes dust, dead skin and loose hairs, prevents serious tangling and matting in long-haired cats and improves circulation. The action of grooming also reveals parasites, cuts, lumps and bumps and other problems. It can improve your bond with your cat, too. Long-haired cats need to be groomed every day to avoid tangled and matted coats, which can cause skin ▶

HEALTH PROBLEMS

Diarrhoea and vomiting

Diarrhoea and vomiting may be caused by a kitten eating unfamiliar or unsuitable food, over-eating, a sudden change in their diet or an infection caused by bacteria or parasites. Your vet can advise you on the best action to take if your kitten is affected.

Ear problems

Ear problems are common in kittens and cats and can affect different parts of the ear. They can be very painful and can cause long-term problems, so seek veterinary advice as soon as you have any concerns.

Dental problems

Dental disease is very common in both young and older cats. It can be painful and often needs surgery or other treatment. Prevention is key, and all kittens will benefit from being gradually introduced to having their teeth cleaned by regular brushing from an early age. All cats should have their teeth examined at least every 12 months and you may wish to talk to your vet about special diets that aim to keep teeth healthy.

Skin problems

Some of the signs that your kitten may have a skin problem include sore or bald patches, spots or scabs, redness and irritation. There are many possible causes of skin problems, including fleas, mites, hormonal changes, allergies and bacterial infections. Always get your kitten checked out by a vet if they show any of these symptoms.

LEFT: Prevent dental disease with regular cleaning and check-ups.

◄ problems. Short-haired cats also benefit from grooming, especially if they are moulting.

Cats that are not groomed regularly may swallow large amounts of hair when they are grooming themselves, which can cause hair balls. Usually the hair passes out of their system, but sometimes a clump of matted hair will form in the gut. Cats often remove the hair ball themselves by vomiting it up; sometimes they eat grass first, which is thought to help them regurgitate the hair. If hair balls are a persistent problem, talk to your vet.

Kittens should be introduced to grooming as early as possible so they become accustomed to it. Choose a quiet time of day when both you and your kitten are feeling relaxed. Make it a positive experience by incorporating toys or tasty treats. Let your kitten approach you, so you don't make them feel trapped or frightened. Start with brief grooming sessions and stop when your kitten shows that they have had enough. Never trim your pet's whiskers, as they are an essential part of your cat's senses.

Keeping your kitten safe at home

Kittens love exploring, so you should make sure their surroundings are safe. Ordinary household items such as pans of boiling water, hot fat, live cables and household cleaning products are very dangerous for kittens and must be kept well out of reach. Some house plants and cut flowers, such as lilies, are poisonous to cats, so keep all plants away from them or be careful what you bring into the house.

Avoid giving your cat rubber bands, ribbon, thread or wool to play with – if they are swallowed, they could become twisted around the kitten's intestines, which can be dangerous.

POISONING The poisoning of a pet is every responsible owner's nightmare. Make sure you are prepared for such an emergency. Preventing your cat from coming into contact with poisonous substances and treating any accidental poisonings quickly and appropriately are important parts of responsible pet ownership.

Common items that are poisonous to cats include paracetamol, lilies, antifreeze, spot-on flea treatments for dogs, slug and snail baits or pellets and decorating materials such as paints, varnishes and glass cleaners.

Signs of poisoning include vomiting, diarrhoea, tremors, seizures, coughing and/or sneezing, difficulty breathing, dehydration and hyperactivity. There is more detailed advice on how to prevent poisonings at www.rspca.org.uk/poisoning.

HAZARDS IN THE GARDEN Your
garden will likely become part of your cat's territory, and they should be free to enjoy it safely. Before your kitten is allowed outside, though, check for hazards.

Some cats enjoy drinking from ponds and water butts, which puts them at risk of falling in. Cover your pond with wire mesh and make sure your water butt has a lid.

Before locking your shed or closing your garage door, always check that your cat hasn't followed you inside – missing cats often turn out to have been accidentally locked in. Ensure that pesticides, fertilizers and other chemicals are stored out of reach. During the winter, keep any de-icing salt out of your cat's reach, as it is toxic to them.

Check that wooden structures such as fences are in good condition with no sharp parts that might injure your cat. Always keep an eye out for your cat when using garden equipment such as lawn mowers.

IN AN EMERGENCY Emergencies can be really scary, but try not to panic.
- Stay calm. If you think your cat has been poisoned, remove them from the source of poison.
- Contact your vet for advice immediately – always phone before taking your cat in, as you may be able to get essential advice over the phone, and you may need to go to a different place than usual.
- Follow your vet's advice. If you are advised to take your cat to the vet, do so quickly and calmly.
- Never attempt to treat or medicate your cat yourself. Some medicines for humans or other animals may be poisonous to your cat.

If you think your kitten has eaten something that will make them ill, never attempt to make them vomit. Do not give them salt water, as this is extremely dangerous.

LEFT TO RIGHT: Make grooming part of your cat's regular routine. Toxic items: decorating materials, a needle and thread.
ABOVE: Slug and snail pellets.

Your questions answered

Alice Potter BSc (Hons) MSc, cat behaviour and welfare expert, Companion Animals Department, RSPCA.

Q: Why does my cat need regular worming treatment?

A: Many kittens have roundworm, because it is commonly passed on to them in their mother's milk. However, most often kittens and cats that have worms don't show any symptoms, so it is not always obvious. This means that having your kitten treated regularly for worms is very important to keep them healthy and happy. If worms are left untreated your kitten may become very unwell. As well as roundworm, there are other worms such as tapeworms that can infect your kitten. Different worms may need different treatments. Always ask your vet to advise on which treatment is safe and suitable for your kitten.

Q: My vet has prescribed tablets for my kitten. What is the best way to give them?

A: The most easy and stress-free way to get your kitten to take tablets is by hiding them in a treat or food. Check with your vet first to make sure the tablet is suitable to be taken with food – many of them are. Wet food or soft, mushy treats work best because the tablet can be buried inside them. If your cat eats around the tablet or spits it out it can be a good idea to crush the tablet and mix it into a small amount of tasty food – again, check with your vet that it is safe to do so. If hiding the tablet in food doesn't work, your vet will be able to advise you on other ways of encouraging your kitten to take their medicine. It

is also important to only use medicines that have been prescribed for your individual kitten.

Q: How do I train my new kitten to use the litter tray?

A: Most kittens learn how to use a litter tray fairly quickly, but some may take longer than others. It is important to place the litter tray away from your kitten's food and water bowls in a quiet, private spot. Never allow your kitten to be disturbed whilst toileting. Make sure

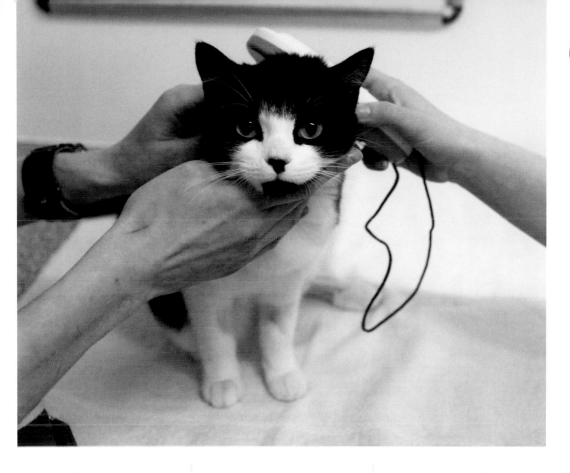

you use the same type of litter that your kitten had at the rehoming centre or breeder's. If you wish to change it, this should be done gradually. Take your kitten to the tray each time they wake from a nap and after every meal. When you see your kitten using the tray, offer a small treat as a reward. Never punish your kitten if they toilet outside the litter tray – your kitten will not understand why they are being punished and it will frighten them. Toileting in the house is often seen in cats and can be caused by a number of factors, including stress, fear, an inappropriate litter tray, environment and health issues. If this continues, it is best to take your cat to the vet for a health check. If necessary your vet may refer you to a qualified animal behaviourist.

Q: Why does my kitten need pet insurance and microchipping?
A: Think about taking out pet insurance and having your cat microchipped. Pet insurance will cover unexpected vet's bills and safeguard your cat's health. A one-off payment for microchipping your cat means you are more likely to be quickly reunited if they go missing.

LEFT: Place your kitten's litter tray in a quiet, private spot. ABOVE: Microchipping means that you are more likely to be reunited if your pet goes missing or is stolen.

Index

Resources

RSPCA

For more information and advice from the RSPCA about caring for your kitten, go to www.rspca.org.uk/cats.

Veterinary advice

- Find a vet: Advice on finding low-cost veterinary care at www.rspca.org.uk/findavet.
- Find a Vet at www.findavet. rcvs.org.uk/home.
- Vet Help Direct at www. vethelpdirect.com.
- Vetfone (24-hour service) at www.vetfone.co.uk.

Behaviour advice

- Advice on finding a behaviourist at www.rspca. org.uk/findabehaviourist.
- The Association for the Study of Animal Behaviour (ASAB) at www.asab.org.
- The Association of Pet Behaviour Counsellors (APBC) at www.apbc.org.uk.
- If you are concerned about your kittens's behaviour, contact a major rescue organization or rehoming centre, such as the RSPCA, for expert advice. They will be happy to help you, even if you have not adopted your pet from their rehoming centres.

PET GUIDE

Learn more about other popular pets with these bestselling RSPCA pet guides